Mark Metcalf, Fred Gwynne (above), John Lithgow and James Greene in a scene from the New York Shakespeare Festival production of "Salt Lake City Skyline." Set designed by Marjorie Kellogg.

SALT LAKE CITY SKYLINE

BY THOMAS BABE

★

DRAMATISTS
PLAY SERVICE
INC.

For my mother, Ruth

SALT LAKE CITY SKYLINE was originally produced by the New York Shakespeare Festival (Joseph Papp, Producer) in January, 1980. It was directed by Robert Allan Ackerman, with scenery by Marjorie Kellogg, costumes by Robert Wojewodsky, and lighting by Arden Fingerhut. The cast, in order of speaking, was:

THE JUDGE .... Fred Gwynne

THE DEFENSE .... Mark Metcalf

THE PROSECUTION .... James Greene

JOE HILL .... John Lithgow

JOHN DAWSON .... Tom McKitterick

OFFICER GRUBER .... Will Patton

ELIZABETH DAWSON .... Gail Strickland

MRS. SEELEY .... Hariet Miller

BAILIFF .... Peter Bosché

MR. JEFFERSON .... Don Plumley

JERUSALEM SLIM .... J. C. Quinn

PRESENT AT THE TRIAL .... Raynor Scheine, Richard Frank, Frank Muller and James Carruthers

4

CHARACTERS

JOE HILL, 40

ELIZABETH DAWSON, the same age, of means

JOHN, her son

THE JUDGE, 60

THE DEFENSE, a smart young lawyer

THE PROSECUTION, settled in his job

JERUSALEM SLIM, Joe's Buddy, 40

WITNESSES:
 OFFICER GRUBER
 MR. JEFFERSON
 MRS. SEELEY

A BAILIFF

The lyrics to the songs in the play were written by Joe Hill, who also composed the music or borrowed period popular melodies. All the songs are in the public domain, and are reprinted in *Songs of Joe Hill* (New York, 1955).

In the original Public Theater production, the "Ballad of Joe Hill" by Alfred Hayes and Earl Robinson was sung at the end by the Judge. The song was used by arrangement with MCA Inc.

Note: In the original production, Joe carried his own guitar, picked it up when he wished, even danced on the tables. The point of this is that the called-for piano may not be necessary. The simpler, throughout, that the production values are, the more the fantastic backs-and-forths of the play will seem easy and not require a realistic justification.

SALT LAKE CITY SKYLINE

ACT ONE

The Courtroom in Salt Lake City—an open and easy place, with a bench for the Judge, and tables for the Defense and the Prosecution. A piano is conveniently present, probably right next to the bench, and this, as much as anything, is an indication that life is simple and breezy in this courtroom. There is the presence of windows, through which the sun shines, or not, and through which the sun sets at the end of the play. At the outset, the Judge takes his place and gavels the proceedings to order.

JUDGE. We now gather for the fourteenth, by my reckoning, day to consider in trial the fate of Mr. Joseph Hillstrom who has been accused by the state of Utah and by its thrifty, industrious inhabitants of a dual homicide, by pistol. The court has taken notice of the fact that a significant labor organization which espouses the doctrines of a Mr. Karl Marx, the Industrial Workers of the World, feels that Mr. Hillstrom, an espousee of the doctrines of the I.W.W. and Mr. Marx, is being unduly persecuted. Our function remains to see that he is duly prosecuted. May we proceed?

DEFENSE. That is going to be difficult since it has become common knowledge that your honor is now, officially, as the *Tribune* informs us today, dying.

JUDGE. I don't see where my mortality is an issue. I expect to survive this trial, survive the appeals, and be here.

DEFENSE. Your judgement may be impaired—

PROSECUTION. Object.

JUDGE. A man may die and yet not be bereft of sense or good judgement in the bargain. I expect, if my mind becomes clouded, I will bow out. In the meantime, Mr. Hill is on trial for murder.

7

JOE. (*Standing.*) Yes sir, and I don't know what good you boys can all do me. My lawyers work for no money and the state, as it calls itself over there, has the benefit of a young army of coppers and tecks and spies and Chinese laundrymen, for all I know. But I do think your honor should be allowed to work because I think the worth of a man is his work and his wages, and I don't want to see you lose a job on account of me. In fact, I think you should make work here, if you can. That's how we get along on our side.

PROSECUTION. I object.

JUDGE. To what?

PROSECUTION. The defendant just made a speech.

DEFENSE. Now, wait a moment, now I object, I absolutely, by God almighty, if there is a God—

PROSECUTION. I object, and the court may take judicial notice of the fact that there is a God—

DEFENSE. I must lodge an objection to the objection, and also much of the flimsy, heresayical, contrived, rehearsed, exaggerated, mud-ball testimony—

PROSECUTION. Mudball?

DEFENSE. I believe you heard me.

PROSECUTION. Object to mudball, whatever that may be?

DEFENSE. A euphemism for horseshit, councilor. (*A woman faints.*)

PROSECUTION. I object to the use of the word "euphemism."

JUDGE. (*Bemused.*) Why?

PROSECUTION. Its meaning eludes me.

DEFENSE. As much has, in the groping for truth in what has thus far been elicited here in what may only be characterized with great charity as a "tabernacle of justice . . ."

PROSECUTION. (*To Judge.*) There, you see, he did it again. I object to the word "tabernacle."

DEFENSE. A man is on trial for his life here.

PROSECUTION. Tabernacle is a prejudicial word. It is meant to reflect on Mormonism. It was put into the record for the purposes of introducing a taint.

JUDGE. Gentlemen! Gentlemen! (*The Judge bangs them to silence. Dawson twirls her parasol, cries out and faints. She is helped as Joe watches.*)

JOE. (*In a dark suit; gaunt and haggard; begins to sing a cappella in a low, rich voice.*)*

* Music for this song, "Rebel Girl," is included at back of playbook.

8

There are women of many descriptions
In this queer world, as everyone knows.
(*He moves to the piano, begins to accompany himself.*)
Some are living in beautiful mansions
And are wearing the finest of clothes.
(*Several voices join him; the Widow Dawson is helped up, given water and smelling salts, during:*)
There are blue-blooded queens and princesses
Who have charms made of diamonds and pearl
But the only and Thoroughbred Lady
Is the Rebel Girl.
(*Widow Dawson opens her parasol and makes to leave. In the refrain, which Joe sings with great passion, those watching and his attornies, and finally even the judge, join in.*)
That's the Rebel Girl. That's the Rebel Girl.
To the working class she's a precious pearl.
She brings courage, pride and joy
To the Fighting Rebel Boy.
We've had girls before
But we need some more
In the Industrial Workers of the World,
For it's great to fight for freedom
With a Rebel Girl.
(*The widow exits, Joe looking after her, longingly. The Judge again gavels.*)
JUDGE. Call your next witness.
PROSECUTION. We call City Police Officer William Gruber.
JUDGE. Officer Gruber? (*The policeman sits in the witness box. The oath is administered sotto voce and in a perfunctory way while we see Joe Hill arguing with his lawyers.*)
GRUBER. . . . so help me God!
HILL. (*Very loud.*) Damn the eyes of the blind lady!
JUDGE. Mr. Hill, are you having a difficulty?
JOE. No more than the usual.
JUDGE. How would you characterize the difficulty?
JOE. It's these characters I have to deal with who allege and detract that they are my lawyers. Why, one of them's so no damn good he got here today with his fly open. (*Lawyer closes his fly.*)
JUDGE. May the court ask you to sit and listen to the testimony given, without prejudicing any of your own interests, so that you may make a defense of yourself later? We have only a common interest in the truth.

9

JOE. Well, if I laughed, what could you do to me? Hang me? That would be a good one.

JUDGE. May I observe . . . ?

JOE. Sure, observe. Do I get to observe?

JUDGE. Later, after the verdict, usually at sentencing, unless you are innocent, in which case your innocence, I presume, will speak with the tongues of the angels.

JOE. I wouldn't know. I'm going the other way.

JUDGE. You have, Mr. Hill, from the outset of these proceedings, shown no interest in your own defense, no interest in the charges against you, and no respect for this court, which, after all, stands between you and a fatally broken neck. The court cannot say why, only surmise the reasons. You may be criminally insane, we have heard testimony that you are of a psychopathic disposition. You may be, certainly, participating in a odor of sainthood, as your own radical newspaper alleges you are. Or you may be, to put this as nicely as possible, a half-cocked jackass. In which case, if you are of the brotherhood of those unfortunately sterile beasts of burden, I must protect you and the state of Utah must protect you and your own lawyers must protect you from stumbling. If you will be, now, so good as to settle onto that chair, we will hear from the police officer. I do not want to have you here bound and gagged just so we can get on with the business.

JOE. Yes, well, I have a very radical idea.

JUDGE. Politics are of no moment.

JOE. No, sir, no, to save myself!

JUDGE. In God's good time.

DEFENSE. We object.

JUDGE. (*Businesslike.*) Over-ruled. God does inhabit vast parts, though not all parts, of this state.

PROSECUTION. (*To Officer Gruber.*) Would you tell us, from your notes, exactly what transpired, Officer Gruber?

GRUBER. (*A little thick.*) Yes sir. On the night of January ten, the year nineteen fourteen, two masked assailant-bandits armed with pistols made into the store of J.G. Morrison, cried out, "We've got you now" and fired several small lead objects, commonly known as bullets, into the store owner and his young son. The owner fell at once, but the lad was able to get off a shot, which wounded one of the predatory bandits. As both father and son lay dying in their own blood—

DEFENSE. Objection.

10

JUDGE. Was it someone else's blood they lay in?
DEFENSE. Inflammatory.
JUDGE. You're darn-tootin' right. Over-ruled.
GRUBER. The bandits fled the scene, leaving gruesome trails of blood. Although we were unable that night to find anyone—
DEFENSE. I object.
JUDGE. (To Gruber.) Very well. Were you able to find anyone that night?
GRUBER. We found someone, six "someones" in fact, but not anyone as to imply consistent guilt.
JUDGE. Overruled. They found *someone,* but not anyone. Proceed.
GRUBER. We subsequently learned that the defendant, Joseph Hillstrom, also known here as Joe Hill, arrived at the surgery of Dr. McHugh two hours after the shooting at the Morrison grocery—
DEFENSE. Object.
JUDGE. To what? All of this is part of the record, Mr. Springhorn. The good doctor has already testified that he saw Mr. Hill.
DEFENSE. Withdrawn.
PROSECUTION. Then Officer Gruber . . . ?
GRUBER. The defendant was treated for one bullet wound, beneath the nipple and grazing the lung. The doctor in question subsequently drove the defendant Hill to the defendant Hill's boarding house where the defendant Hill was apprehended after having been drugged with morphine, but while reaching for a pistol under his pillow—
DEFENSE. Object.
GRUBER. There was no pistol under his pillow: we presumed there was a pistol under his pillow. Because the defendant was very weak, from the prior wound to his chest and also his hand, he offered no resistance. He was thereby taken into custody and we threw him in jail, not the hospital, because I suppose we hoped the son-of-a-bitch would die on us and save the trial.
DEFENSE. I Object.
JUDGE. The court recognizes that the contention that the defendant is a son-of-a-female dog is not documented and cannot be. Strike from the record.
GRUBER. He had a gun when he arrived at the doctor's and he threw the gun away on the traversing motor journey home after he was treated.

11

PROSECUTION. Has the defendant, Joe Hill, ever accounted for the gunshot wound he sustained on the same night as the awful hold-up and murders?

GRUBER. He did.

PROSECUTION. Did he not tell you that he had been shot in a quarrel about a lady?

DEFENSE. Object.

PROSECUTION. And if that *is* true, Officer Gruber, do you know where the lady is?

DEFENSE. I object, and object, and object again. The prosecution is leading its own witness.

JUDGE. We have heard much throughout this trial about "the lady." You can object to the question, of course. Personally I object to being kept in the dark about the *femme fatale*. Is there anything else?

DEFENSE. Officer Gruber, do you have any specific feelings about the defendant?

GRUBER. No more than most, sir. He's a hobo, a radical terrorist, and he writes namby-pamby songs about down-and-outs with no trade or craft wanting jobs. European sorts, like himself, and coons.

DEFENSE. Move to strike except as tending to show prejudice.

JUDGE. Sustained. (*To Gruber.*) Excused. (*To Prosecution.*) What do we have now?

PROSECUTION. Your honor, the bawdy hand of the dial, so to speak, is on the prick of one, and I think we could all profit from a midday repast.

JUDGE. The court stands adjourned until three.

JOE. Your honor—!

JUDGE. (*Paternally.*) Till three, Joe, then we can all get together again, as we have these last few days, and squabble this out.

JOE. (*Nicely.*) Thank you, your honor. (*The court room empties. Joe Hill alone with John Dawson, who brings him a picnic basket and a guitar. The two eat cold chicken, bread, and drink coffee, during:*)

JOHN. (*Proffering the basket.*) Mom said to bring you.

JOE. Thank you, kindly.

JOHN. You think they had you by the tail then?

JOE. No, their case has nothing to it. They do carry on, though, don't they?

JOHN. You think you're being hurt?

JOE. No.

JOHN. I'm not hardly a person to judge these things, but you were hurt.

JOE. No. Justice will save me.

JOHN. You don't allow for justice to exist, you said. For the working stiffs.

JOE. Well, some of that was my adding a little salt and pepper to a flat meal. I suppose the courts must work, at least.

JOHN. You do?

JOE. I suppose so. Everything can't be as bad as I say it is. The bosses can run everything, but they don't run the courts.

JOHN. You were hurt there.

JOE. Well, all this food your mam sends me and the money for the defense, I don't think any one body is worth this kind of trouble, though I'm thankful. Say, how's your mam?

JOHN. Good. I mean, excellent for being sad.

JOE. You tell her to keep a strong look in her eye.

JOHN. I think if you're found guilty, I might blow up the state capital building and the governor's mansion.

JOE. That's no good. But if you do it, make sure you do it right, cause I've known some fine old boys who didn't use enough fuse or didn't run fast enough.

JOHN. (Angry.) I mean it.

JOE. I know you mean it. There's a better way, though. When I landed in San Francisco, they gave me a job which would've lasted me about eight hours while the bosses would've pocketed my labor. We were supposed to unload a shipment of shingles from a railroad siding to wagons and trucks . . . twenty thousand bundles of two hundred shingles each, and would you believe, some criminal, radical type had cut the iron band around every single bundle. I don't know who could've done it, but when our boss saw the situation, and had exhausted his supply of curse words . . . he told us to re-bundle all twenty thousand bundles. We got six days work out of that little episode and nicked, I believe, three hundred dollars from the shingle profits. (Pause.) If they kill me, don't be a damn fool. Go cut their hearts out by inches. Don't mourn. Organize.

JOHN. I never organized a thing.

JOE. You'll learn.

JOHN. I don't want to. You know, I was never taken to fish by anyone. I was taken to school and church by my ma, and to an association for the improvement of juvenile youths by my father.

You took me to fish the first time I ever was taken. You let me smoke tobacco. You said I shouldn't, but you let me and we set in the grass and talked about nothing at all I can remember, which was nice, because I remember we dropped a line and talked about nothing I can remember.

JOE. You make chin music like a regular homeless hobo these days.

JOHN. I wish this wouldn't happen.

JOE. It might.

JOHN. Cause you let it.

JOE. I don't know.

JOHN. You do. You could stop it. I'll be very angry if you let it happen.

JOE. You'll get over it.

JOHN. You don't seem to care!

JOE. Oh, I do. I like this chicken very well. I like coffee and donuts, that's pretty much what you get, but if you can share them with some of the boys, the good bunch, then you have what you need. Some of them, like you, have the craziest ideas for good boys, which is to live in cabins in the hills and raise their own food. That's nothin' to holler about. There's more to all this than fishing. But I love this chicken so very well, your mam knows.

JOHN. (*Suddenly standing, angry.*) I hope you rot because you've got no right, no right at all, to take away all you gave me. (*Joe picks up the guitar and strums.*)

JOE. (*Speaks over strumming, rhythmically.*) And when the moon was shining bright/they kept me working all the night/one moonlit-night, I hate to tell/I "accidentally" slipped and fell./My pitchfork went right in between/some cog wheels of the thresh machine./ And . . . (*Sings, to the tune of the old song "Ta-Ra-Ra-Boom De-Ay."*) Ta-ra-ra-boom-de-ay
It made a noise that way
And wheels and bolts and hay
Went flying every way.
That stingy rube said, "Well!
A thousand gone to hell."
But I did sleep that night,
I needed it all right.
   (*Pauses.*)

JOHN. So why did you kill old Morrison and his son?

JOE. You concluded that I did, then?

14

JOHN. You must've done lots of things I don't know anything about. You might've had to kill them for a good reason. Some people think you're like Robin Hood.

JOE. Him? He was an English fellow lived in a forest. Most people nowdays live in the industrial centers.

JOHN. They don't have to.

JOE. (*Laughs; then tough.*) Tell your mam not to come to the court anymore if she can help it. I get distracted. (*John grabs up the picnic things and the courtroom suddenly fills with the attornies and the judge.*)

JUDGE. Gentlemen. Mr. Hill.

JOE. Your honor?

JUDGE. You had an objection to lodge before the break.

JOE. I think it's slipped my mind. I was eating some good food here.

JUDGE. Which disrupted your train of thought? Are you a sensualist, Mr. Hill?

JOE. Your Honor?

JUDGE. Enjoy things? You seem to have had a hard life, whatever else you have done or not.

JOE. Would it be I should say I'm a sensualist socialist and then all the spelling would confuse people?

JUDGE. No, I was curious, Mr. Hill. I don't want to preside over your demise if you are actually innocent. I don't want to kill you, so you should not make me. (*Pause.*) Counsellors, may we proceed?

PROSECUTION. Call Mrs. Seeley.

JOE. She's a highly unreliable type. A snoopy type. Lives in misery. (*Oath administered during:*)

JUDGE. You don't have anything against women, do you, Mr. Hill?

JOE. Just the nattering ones. Mostly they scare the beans out of me.

JUDGE. Have you ever been married? (*Pause.*) Or who was it, the mystery woman of your unexpressed defense?

SEELEY. (*At the end of the oath being administered.*) "I do."

PROSECUTION. Mrs. Seeley, we want to do this in an orderly fashion. We want to allow you to relax and recall. On the evening of the murders at the Morrison grocery, you saw two men walking shoulder to shoulder away from the store who crowded you off the street.

SEELEY. I did.

PROSECUTION. Did this man that turned, the taller of the two, did he look directly at you?

SEELEY. Yes.

PROSECUTION. And did you look directly at him?

SEELEY. Yes.

PROSECUTION. Did you notice anything peculiar about the features of the face of the man . . . ?

SEELEY. Yes.

PROSECUTION. I wish you would tell, in your own way, Mrs. Seeley, what there was about the face of the man that attracted your attention.

SEELEY. Well, his face was real thin; he had a sharp nose and rather large nostrils. He had a defect on the side of his face or neck.

JOE. A scar.

SEELEY. You'd say, yes.

JUDGE. Mr. Hill!

JOE. I'm an impatient man, your honor, and I thought I'd help her along.

PROSECUTION. Defect on the side of the face or neck?

SEELEY. Right here on his face.

PROSECUTION. And it might be a scar?

SEELEY. Yes.

PROSECUTION. Did the nose appear to be particularly sharp?

SEELEY. Yes.

PROSECUTION. And the nostrils were peculiar?

SEELEY. Yes, the gentleman that I met was a sharp-faced man with a real sharp nose, a disfiguration on the face or neck, and his nostrils were rather large. And I will never forget the eyes.

PROSECUTION. Why?

SEELEY. I don't know. I have never met eyes like those. I thought they were clear, real clear like water, but they were hard. (*Pointing to Hill.*) Like his eyes, very much.

PROSECUTION. Nothing further.

JUDGE. Cross-examine?

DEFENSE. Mrs. Seeley, is it your belief the man you saw and the defendant, Mr. Hill, are one and the self-same?

SEELEY. There is a great deal of similarity in the nose holes, the scar and the sharp face, yes. And the eyes.

DEFENSE. So that's it?

SEELEY. Yes.

DEFENSE. No further questions.

JOE. See if it was snowing.

DEFENSE. Snowing?

JOE. Ask her! Snow does funny things to a person. Ask her!

DEFENSE. Was it snowing, Mrs. Seeley?

SEELEY. It had just, and might still have been. The wind *was* blowing.

DEFENSE. Which meant you had to be walking with your head down.

SEELEY. I never walk with my head down, sir.

DEFENSE. No more questions.

JOE. No. Ask her if the cold and snow numbed her brains.

DEFENSE. Joe, I can't. It's a stupid question. It'll only make things worse.

JOE. Ask her if she blabbed a hundred different stories about all this.

DEFENSE. Joe, I won't conduct a cross-examination blind. You've got to trust me.

JOE. No! Ask her if she couldn't remember before. Ask her why she remembers so well now. Ask her if she'd been coached by the railroad engineers who are running the prosecution.

JUDGE. Mr. Hill, it is outburst after outburst with you. Your attorneys will handle your defense. *(To Seeley.)* Excused. *(To Joe.)* If it is, as you say, impossible for you to have been where the sturdy and honest Mrs. Seeley apparently thinks you were on the night of the killings, then you have only to say where you were, which specific place allowed you to tryst, fight, get shot, and develop that look Mrs. Seeley has described that is certainly in your eyes.

JOE. May I say a few words?

JUDGE. You have the right to be heard in your own behalf.

JOE. I have two prosecuting attorneys here and . . . *(Pointing to his own defense lawyer.)* I intend to get rid of one of them. You sit over there, you are fired, too, see. And there is something I don't understand . . .

JUDGE. You need not carry out in detail any difference you may have with counsel, if any.

JOE. I wish to announce I have discharged my counsel, my lawyers.

DEFENSE. Since you've discharged us, that's all there is to it.

JOE. If the court will permit, I will act as my own attorney after this, and cross-examine all the witnesses, and I think I will make a good job of it. As far as the district attorney is concerned, I think we get along fine; he comes right out in the middle of the road. These fellows . . . (*Indicating his own attorneys.*) I think I can get along very nicely without them.

JUDGE. You realize it is a remarkable proceeding, at least, to get up in the midst of a trial and discharge your counsel.

JOE. Well, I do. I'd thought this was going to be a lark because I thought I could stand up here and say I didn't kill a soul and I never have and you would look at me and believe me. But now it seems not to be going well and I will be convicted for my nostrils here and my inclination to sing radical songs for those who have the wholly unnatural instinct to want to eat and feed their own. So it seems I cannot appeal to any conscience without being reasonable and legal. But I am going to be vindicated, or die trying.

JUDGE. Vindicated of what? Having large nostrils? A flair for music? This is a murder trial. You stand accused, Mr. Hill, as nothing much more or less than a common thug. That is the issue.

JOE. Yes, I know, that, that is what I meant.

JUDGE. I think we must retire to chambers to discuss this. But I have just been handed a message, Mr. Hill, from the president of the United States who has asked this court, in his name, to use its full authority to guarantee you a fair trial, and, by God, that's what you will get, like it or not. (*The court room clears; Joe alone a moment. He breaks a pencil in anger. Elizabeth Dawson enters.*)

DAWSON. What difference does it make how you get free?

JOE. (*Startled.*) I thought I told your boy to keep you off this courtroom.

DAWSON. Could I? (*They both smile.*)

JOE. I have my doubts.

DAWSON. I've talked to my husband.

JOE. The son-of-a-bitch shot me.

DAWSON. Well, he wanted to.

JOE. I know, but I didn't have my pants on even.

DAWSON. We were supposed to be moving along quickly, but you dawdled on the way.

JOE. Well, I don't have much acquaintance with charm like yours that I wished to rush it.

DAWSON. Things will have to change, anyway, according to you. We shall all soon be living in a world where we all eat off the same table, and you won't be so smart anymore. And I won't be so fine and dandy.

JOE. I know what you think. I came around, and you listened, and

18

you have money, yes, my lady, you have a position, and I think I must've seemed very nice to you and my opinions were very interesting and exciting and I think you wanted the love of my opinions and my colorful life because the stories were so good and the songs and because you were flattered that a dangerous radical would touch you in certain places, including on your body. But things don't change, otherwise, despite what I say and hope.

DAWSON. What do you think? A man of means like my husband comes to his home and finds a ragged wobbly agitator with his pants down lying nearly on top of his wife? The least he could do would be to shoot you. And the least I can do is to sit up there and say he did it.

JOE. I wouldn't let you.

DAWSON. Why do you think I couldn't love you?

JOE. Because when you say love, m'lady, you mean that you had a certain kind of fun with me and you got very sentimental about the fun. I did, too. But that's not enough to make a life of. You have your other obligations, however-so-much fun you had with me.

DAWSON. Well, I wouldn't be ruined forever if I sat up there and told the truth. True, I wouldn't be invited to some social events, I would be snubbed, I might even have to transport my fading earthly beauty to some other territory, but I won't die. I was rather proud of us, in a way.

JOE. Why?

DAWSON. Because I liked us, the idea of us. I certainly did like you.

JOE. That's bull-dickie and you know it. You had a lust.

DAWSON. Didn't you?

JOE. I don't know I want to be liked because I'm lusted.

DAWSON. You must have been lusted before.

JOE. Well . . . I don't like to think.

DAWSON. I'm going to sit down beside you and hold your hand. (*She does so; a moment of silence.*)

JOE. I have no truck with Bibles. They promise you a better life when none is left to you. But I like the stories a whole hell of a lot. Eve bit the apple, and I'm gonna write a song about that, if they don't hang me.

DAWSON. She made the fellow bite the apple. So, what went wrong there?

JOE. Well, the fellow, as you call him, got interested in his own

19

delights, and he forgot the rest. He was a damn fool. (*Joe turns and kisses Dawson. They kiss lightly a moment and then kiss hard. Joe's hands begin to move over the widow's body.*) I do love you, Elizabeth, so you can satisfy that curiosity. I wish I could say with a straight face, "May God help me!" (*They kiss again. John enters the room, stops, stares. Joe, pausing a moment in the kiss:*) Don't just stand there, son, come on in, I'll get to explaining when I've finished being sinful. (*Dawson bolts away; sits up; adjusts her hair.*)

JOHN. (*After a moment.*) So why is it I'm considered to be stupid, Mr. Hill?

JOE. Not stupid. Just lacking certain knowledge of the world's ways.

JOHN. People like to hug and kiss.

JOE. Some people.

JOHN. Everybody, it seems.

JOE. Well, somebody all the time, yes, and everybody some of the time.

JOHN. But nobody none of the time.

JOE. You haven't been watching the judge, Johnny.

JOHN. He hugs and kisses himself. So does everybody who hasn't got somebody sometime or everybody, like you, all the time.

JOE. I don't have anything and I think you should say a gracious greeting to your mother.

JOHN. She has a few bodies most of the time. Damn, that doesn't matter.

JOE. I don't think you should say damn to the face of your mother.

DAWSON. I can speak for myself. And I must say, to the both of you, there is a matter of principle at stake here. Mr. Hill represents a movement of great dimension and force and he should not be executed. I think he should do and become what he chooses, and so, John, I am going to testify on Mr. Hill's behalf, that the bullet wound he received was inflicted by a jealous husband and father who apprehended us in *flagrante delicto,* and that Mr. Hill was with *me* when the awful murders transpired.

JOE. I'm not even going to let you testify to your shoe size.

DAWSON. You can't stop me.

JOE. Sure I can. I can say you're a liar and I can say I don't know you and I can say, here, I don't love you. I can do that.

DAWSON. Why?

JOE. Because I don't want to hurt anyone, except, if need be, myself, and because I want to be acquitted not for the facts but because they look at me, they look me square in the eye, and say, Mr. Joseph Hillstrom, we like you, we take your word you might not be a killer.

JOHN. Yeah . . . and? That lady Seeley took one look in your eye that night, and she said she'd never forget it.

JOE. It wasn't me. Elizabeth I appreciate the offer of the alibi, but Joe Hill doesn't alibi.

DAWSON. (*Angry.*) You stupid son-of-a-bitch.

JOE. That was a harsh thing to say.

JOHN. You double stupid son-of-a-bitch, I hope they hang you higher than the skyline.

DAWSON. John, Mr. Hill would like that, but we mustn't hope for it. (*The court returns and Dawson draws away.*)

JUDGE. We are ready to proceed. Mr. Hill, it is the court's estimation that you can represent yourself, but I have asked your attorneys, Mr. Springhorn and Mr. Smith, to remain as friends of the court.

JOE. They may be friends of yours—

JUDGE. Call your first witness.

JOE. Well, I see Mr. Jefferson there, can I call Mr. Jefferson?

JUDGE. You may subpoena anyone in the court.

JOE. Mr. Jefferson. (*A portly Mr Jefferson takes the stand, uncomfortable, and the oath is administered.*)

JEFFERSON. I do. I have no notion of why I was called since I know nothing of any details of these killings.

JOE. I called you to be a character witness.

JEFFERSON. I don't think much of your character.

JOE. I wanted to know about yours.

PROSECUTION. Objection.

JUDGE. Sustained.

JOE. What do you do for a living, Mr. Jefferson?

PROSECUTION. Objection.

JUDGE. On what grounds?

PROSECUTION. Generally.

JUDGE. Over-ruled. Continue. You will answer the question.

JEFFERSON. I manage the Number Twenty-seven mine in Demarest.

JOE. And why did you come to the trial?

PROSECUTION. Objection.

JUDGE. Well, I want to know, too. He should be managing the mine if he's a mine-manager. Answer the question.

JEFFERSON. I was just curious, like the others, to see if he'd get away with it.

JOE. With what?

PROSECUTION. Objection.

JOE. You have a lot of objections.

JUDGE. Sustained. Where are we going, Mr. Hill?

JOE. (*Confused a moment.*) I don't know, precisely . . .

PROSECUTION. Objection.

JOE. Now he's objecting to my ignorance.

JUDGE. Over-ruled. Proceed.

JOE. Do you know me, Mr. Jefferson?

PROSECUTION. Objection.

JUDGE. Will you sit down a minute and shut up? Proceed.

JEFFERSON. I can say I do. You did some work for me. You were a good worker, as workers go, and you could still be there if you wanted, but I can't say I know you.

JOE. Is it true I was paid seven dollars for those weeks, each week?

JEFFERSON. True.

JOE. Is it true that the company paid for everything of mine and that I ran a bill at the store?

JEFFERSON. Most do.

JOE. Is it true that every week I went and you gave me the bill which said lodging two dollars, food three dollars, tobacco and liquor one dollar, and clothing one dollar?

JEFFERSON. That's a sound approximation of the usual.

JOE. Is it also true that there was an extra charge of fifty cents for medical insurance?

JEFFERSON. That's standard.

JOE. So what do you make it, my bill?

JEFFERSON. That'd be seven fifty a week.

JOE. So every week I had to pay you fifty cents to work out there.

JEFFERSON. Right.

PROSECUTION. Objection, again in general, to all of this.

JUDGE. Sustained.

JEFFERSON. The point being, your honor—

JUDGE. You have been objected to and sustained.

JEFFERSON. Well, I had something to say.

JUDGE. (*To prosecution.*) Do you want to take him on cross?

22

PROSECUTION. With delight. He is Mr. Hill's witness.

JOE. I object.

JUDGE. To what?

JOE. Like him, in general.

JUDGE. Over-ruled. Proceed.

PROSECUTION. You indicated, Mr. Jefferson, that you wished to amplify your remarks.

JEFFERSON. Only to stay, and I am cursed to Christmas if I know how any of this has anything to do with cold-blooded murder, he wasn't paying fifty cents there to work for us. He was fed and clothed and sheltered and given medicine and tobacco and red-eye . . .

JOE. (*In a sing-song voice.*) I don't drink. And I don't smoke. I don't lie, nor tell a risque joke.

JUDGE. Notice taken.

JEFFERSON. And for fifty cents extra he got to see the doc once in a while. We did him, and people like him, with no abilities, a favor to give them the employment, and I think the radical angle is way off because these men are shiftless good for-nothings any-way, and this way, you'd think, we keep them from having to rob and kill people to get along.

PROSECUTION. Thank you.

JOE. Objection.

JUDGE. Do you want to try re-direct?

JOE. Sure, whatever the Jesus that is.

JUDGE. Ask him some more questions, Mr. Kinruder will object and I will sustain most of his objections, except where I get un-manageably interested in your line of inquiry.

JOE. Okay, that sounds fair. Mr. Jefferson, do you think my radicalism, as you call it, isn't a real thing?

PROSECUTION. Objection.

JUDGE. You opened the door.

PROSECUTION. Withdrawn.

JUDGE. More music.

JOE. Well . . . ?

JEFFERSON. I think it's like a new hat.

JOE. So if a man feels a certain kin with people who work hard and don't make enough and are always weary and die early and sadly and alone, who got no pleasure out of their lives except to pay you to work, people with some capacities to have feelings and inspire feelings, you think to know that is like wearing a new hat?

23

JEFFERSON. To *you* it is. There *are* some people now really hurting in the slow times.

PROSECUTION. Should I object?

JUDGE. Why? The defendant is really arguing the prosecution's case rather well.

JOE. I just have another question here. How much do you make by the week?

JEFFERSON. Twenty-five dollars.

JOE. Do you do more for your twenty-five than I did for my seven?

JEFFERSON. You're damn right. I have to keep track of all you. That takes character and insight and I'm bein' paid for that, and also, I was born in this country, in this state and I believe in Jesus.

JOE. I guess. He was a hobo rabbi, like me. That's all. (*As Jefferson returns to his seat.*)

PROSECUTION. Move to strike all the foregoing testimony.

JUDGE. Sustained. Mr. Hill, somewhere along the way you and I are going to have to talk—not about the law, songwriting or the activities of the Industrial Workers of the World. We are going to have to discover how you got so far off the track. That will be later, it will be a fruitful conversation, after I have sentenced you. Your next witness?

JOE. I don't know that I know who to call that knows something, but Officer Gruber is likely, so I call Officer Gruber.

JUDGE. Police Officer Gruber? (*Gruber takes the stand.*)

JOE. I want you to tell me, officer, some things you know about this crime.

GRUBER. What?

JOE. I mean, you must have some ideas.

GRUBER. It's not my job to have ideas and opinions.

JOE. So when you solve a crime like this to your level best, you don't think it's one thing or another.

GRUBER. It's murder, two in fact.

JOE. But you don't just think it was done by somebody, but it was done by somebody like somebody, like me.

GRUBER. Well, you did it.

JOE. When you went to the store and walked in, did something there tell you Joe Hill killed this man and his son?

GRUBER. No, that was later.

JOE. When?

GRUBER. Later, when we figured out you did it.

24

JOE. How did you know I did?
GRUBER. How could you not've?
JOE. What about those other six fellows you arrested the same night, why were they let go?
GRUBER. Cause they couldn't've done it.
JOE. So, only I could've done it and not those other six, including two who had bullet wounds they couldn't explain.
GRUBER. But they were just town people, they weren't the sort.
JOE. I didn't strike you as the saint sort of person?
GRUBER. (*Appealing to the Judge.*) I'm having a great deal of difficulty, your honor, answering some or all of these questions because he's asking me things that are not a part of my work.
JUDGE. I think he is trying to ascertain your motive in apprehending *him*, say, rather than any of the other able-bodied men in Salt Lake City who had unexplained bullet holes in *them*.
GRUBER. Because he couldn't explain anything about getting shot, because he looked like the stick-up artist and because he comes from the class of people who do things like this.
JUDGE. (*To Joe, sarcastically.*) Your witness?
JOE. Well, I think, what color shoes was I wearing?
GRUBER. How do I know?
JOE. How about my eye color?
GRUBER. They look bluish.
JOE. What color were they the night of the robbery?
GRUBER. I don't know, Mr. Hill. I wasn't there.
JOE. What do you think of my face?
PROSECUTION. Objection.
JUDGE. Sustained.
JOE. I . . . don't have another question I can think of.
JUDGE. Good. (*To Gruber.*) Excused. If that's the case for the defense, I think we will have summations and then let the jury retire.
PROSECUTION. I don't think much has to be added to the record by my remarks. The man did it, look at him, and he has no defense except that someone is picking on him. An odd defense for cold-blooded murder, and a disgrace even to the movement he claims to represent, as unsavory as that movement is to good Utahans.
JUDGE. Mr. Hill?
JOE. (*Speaking as the introduction to a song.*)
A little girl was working in a big department store,

25

Her little wage for food was spent; her dress was old and tore.
She asked the foreman for a raise, so humbly and so shy,
And this, is what the foreman did reply:
    (*Singing, with the piano.*)
Why don't you get a beau?
Some nice old man, you know!
He'll give you money if you treat him right.
If he has lots of gold
Don't mind if he's old.
Go! Get some nice old gentleman tonight.
    (*Speaking.*) That's my case.
JUDGE. The song cannot exonerate you.
JOE. The man who wrote that, myself, could not kill.
JUDGE. The sentiments are monstrous and cynical. The jury will retire.
JOE. With the permission of the court, I haven't done anything.
JUDGE. (*Calmly.*) That is not quite the case. (*The court is cleared and Joe is alone.*)
JOE. (*To himself.*) Well, old dodger, rebel, raffles, how'd you do it for so long, stay just ahead of them, an inch ahead all the time and now what do you think, they might find you innocent. Maybe it would be better to get around their fancy verdicts, right now, and cut a wrist with a piece of glass, or jump off this court building or throw yourself into the river, the part where its runs a little fast and you'd break up on the rocks, or get a nice lady to buy some strichnine or a gentleman, cyanide—I have friends—even a rifle of the large bore so there couldn't be a mistake, choke yourself on the rope made of the stinking sheets in the jail 'cause you wet them in the night, or maybe go the other way, and take off all of Elizabeth's clothing and push her down in the grass and hurt her with kisses. I don't know, dodger, what's got itself left in the middle? Write a song about it, maybe? Maybe. (*Pause.*) I guess I don't want to do this death of mine as much as I thought I could bear it before. That's a funny aspect for a man as proud as I been.
(*The court returns.*)
JUDGE. May I have the verdict? (*Reading.*) Mr. Joseph Hillstrom has been found guilty of murder in the first and extreme degree on two separate specifications. Sentencing is set for a session tomorrow.
JOE. (*Ashen, rises.*) May I say something?
JUDGE. Not now. Tomorrow. When you walked in here to this

trial, I thought you an interesting and slightly bewildered sort, not handsome and your songs are not all that good, Mr. Hill, but an interesting man. A jury of your peers has just told me that you are a homicidal hoodlum and since I must harken to them, as they are your peers, I don't wish further intercourse with you at this time.

JOE. Now, I want to tell you! I want to give you the reason for the bullet hole! I want to get out of here!

JUDGE. (*Nicely.*) One way or the other, yes. Get a good night's rest. (*Joe is shackled and left at the defense table alone as we blackout.*)

ACT TWO

The courtroom again, near dawn. Joe is still in handcuffs and asleep in the largest stack of law books, open, closed, folded over, crazily-stacked, that anyone has ever seen. A cock crows; he sits up suddenly. Wearily he shuffles through a pile of notes and legal papers while singing to "Tara-ra-boom-deyay.")

JOE.
Res ipsa loquitor
Res gestae, you old whore
O motive, means, and more
Opportunity is de rigor.
Habeaus corpus was no more
When Abe Lincoln ran the war
In rem proceedings just before
Joe Hill outside the door.
(Suddenly the drapes are drawn by the Bailiff and the room flooded with light. The Defense enters. The Bailiff undoes the cuffs and Joe shaves during the following. To his lawyer:) If the law were an instrument of justice, boys, I don't know why she had to be so windy and obtuse in the writing of her.
DEFENSE. For unmistakeable clarity.
JOE. You know there's a precedent for nearly every damn piece of evidence against me to be ridden out of town?
DEFENSE. Not precisely. There are possibilities. But it's perhaps not a good idea for a layman to dabble in the law.
JOE. Or a lawman to get a lay? I'm having a lot of trouble understanding you people.
DEFENSE. You fired us, Joe. We're trying to save you against your own better judgement.
JOE. No, I mean with your education and your kind concern you could probably save a whole bunch of people at one fell swoop instead of minding about one person like me.
DEFENSE. We were assigned the case. I don't have opinions about you or what you belong to or whom you lay.
JOE. No, I can't see that, because everybody has feelings.

28

DEFENSE. I have a feeling, just one, that you want to implead Elizabeth Dawson into these proceedings to save your backside.

JOE. Maybe I did have that feeling yesterday.

DEFENSE. Well, what about today?

JOE. Yesterday I got scared I was really going to get killed by the State of Utah.

DEFENSE. And today, you don't think you'll get your neck broke?

JOE. Today, I just don't know. I don't think it is particularly manful to be afraid of death.

DEFENSE. So do we bring her in, or keep her out?

JOE. I dunno, I'm ashamed to say. I guess I don't much want to die. But I don't want to dishonor anyone and I don't want anybody ever to say, Well, he wasn't a true rebel or son of a rebel, he was a damn goat who wanted to get up the inside of any skirt around, into any pair of pants he could, one of those sort, and they'll say, well, we know what the International Workers of the World are—sex-demented mad people.

DEFENSE. Well, as I see it, you can confess to being a goat, as you put it, in public and everybody will know, and you can live a long life of goathood, or you can keep your being the goat you claim to be a secret, and in three days, you'll be a dead goat, executed by the state.

JOE. But I'm not a goat. I've hardly done anything ever.

DEFENSE. I don't care.

JOE. But, the point is, you see, I've had a passion all my life for most every person, except for those who were unusually cruel or went out of their way to inflict harm; every person, from my mom and pop and brothers and sisters to Aunt Hedda, Gaylik, Marta, some imbecile hurt in a railway smash-up, could have been Fred, I think it was, the Colsons, and then Elizabeth Crawford and Elizabeth Morton, and Elizabeth Ann Vockevec, and Mary Elizabeth Haddad, and Elizabeth Dawson and there must have been a dozen Jims and eight Susans and two Rebeccas, one married, so I just watched her from a distance, and sixteen fellows of mine that had the names of Butch and Boxcar and Curls and Bandana and Slims—Nebraska Slim, Colorado Slim, even Brooklyn Slim, weighed 200 pounds, and Jerusalem Slim. And Nancy I forget her last name, and even her mother, if you want to know, and even her younger sister. (*Pause.*) You couldn't sleep at night if you were me for the things in my head.

DEFENSE. So what do we do?

29

JOE. I don't know.

DEFENSE. You have a choice.

JOE. I didn't know that?

DEFENSE. You can get hung by the neck, till dead, or shot.

JOE. That's very game.

DEFENSE. You can also produce Elizabeth Dawson.

JOE. What would you think of me if I hid behind a woman's skirt?

DEFENSE. Frankly, I wouldn't care. It's going to look bad for me to lose this case, but I can always say, which I always will, that my client would not cooperate, that he spoke of a phantom alibi, he told me there was another reason he got shot but he declined to produce the evidence through a combination of valor and stupidity, and I'll be off the hook. Frankly, I don't think this woman would testify anyway, and I'm not certain I've believed you all along.

JOE. So now I'm a goat, or a liar, but I can't be both and haven't got a hope in hell of being honorable?

DEFENSE. How you choose to go, I guess, the rope or the rifle. Facing a firing squad is more honorable.

JOE. So you got nothing on the line here?

DEFENSE. Don't push me, Joe. I'm tired of this case and tired of you, and if you read all those legal books—

JOE. I did, every damn one!

DEFENSE. You'd know you'd gotten a good defense.

JOE. Well, I'm tempted to do something stupid.

DEFENSE. Something else? What, for Christ's sake?

JOE. Die on you.

DEFENSE. It won't be on me.

JOE. Yep. It'll be on you and him, the prosecutor, and the judge, and every member of the jury that put me there, and the newspapers who put me there, and the governor, and the copper bosses, and every lying member of the crew who testified against me.

DEFENSE. So you're gonna die to hurt the rest of us.

JOE. I might.

DEFENSE. In that case, I want to bash you on both sides of your head, to get my hurt in before you get yours in and are buried six-feet under.

JOE. I might resist.

DEFENSE. Oh, yes? (*Joe puts up his dukes and holds a John L. Sullivan pose. The Defense looks at him a moment, then hauls off and belts him hard in the face. Joe goes sprawling backward into the piles of law books as the Judge enters alone. Joe looks up from the table at the Judge, who peers down a second.)*

JUDGE. Gentlemen?

JOE. We got into a heated exchange about a procedural point.

JUDGE. Your attorney entered a motion?

JOE. Yes, sir, toward my cranium.

JUDGE. I take it the motion was sustained.

JOE. He packs some wallop.

JUDGE. Does he owe you one more? It is usual for an attorney with a client like you to promise two blows to the head.

JOE. Yes sir, he's got one more coming, but next time I might return the favor.

JUDGE. Why, Mr. Hill? You have stained his conscience. *(Pause.)* Mr. Springhorn, I want all the attornies in chambers. My doctors have told me now that I am a much sicker man than I had first been told and that whatever it is that I have is pretty much, to use their words, taking my body like Sherman took Georgia. You can imagine that I am not happy about this, and I'm afraid I must confer with you as to the advisability of my sentencing Mr. Hill, as opposed to someone who is healthier, and therefore, perhaps, less bitter. May we retire? I find my energy flags easily.

JOE. *(Touched.)* But not a red flag, I'll bet.

JUDGE. No, Joe, some red, some white, some blue.

JOE. Damn if that isn't my flag, too.

JUDGE. *(To the Defense.)* Mr. Springhorn! *(The Defense and the Judge retire. Joe begins to clean up his law books and research as Jerusalem Slim, an old crony, in faded work clothes with a huge battered hat, enters. Slim watches Joe a minute scribbling on a legal pad.)*

SLIM. *(Singing softly, Joe looks up.)*
Just a closer walk with thee
Grant it, Jesus, is my plea
Daily walking close with thee
O, let it be, dear Lord, o, let it be.

JOE. *(Annoyed.)* Jerusalem Slim, are you still singing those hogshit songs?

SLIM. *(Annoyed, also.)* I think I had better, Joe Hill, and I always will. *(They both suddenly break out laughing and embrace warmly. Slim makes himself to home, props his feet up on the defense table, moving Joe's books.)* Some of the boys up and down the line were asking for you on the account of what we read in the union papers and the scab

31

papers. so we held up a company store in Duluth and they gave me the proceeds, since I won the draw, to come and see you, inquire after your health, if you'll be needing anything. And I got voted to ask you, even though I didn't want to, but I guess somebody has to and I know even the big shots in our own union won't ask you.

JOE. Which is what?

SLIM. You gonna let them kill you or are you gonna make a defense, as it was implied you might?

JOE. I'm set down to be murdered day after tomorrow.

SLIM. You ain't been finally sentenced, though. I just heard the learned judge. (*Pause. Joe doesn't answer the question.*)

JOE. Well, we had some good times anyway, right, Slim?

SLIM. Didn't we? I been in ten jails with you, had my head busted four times—

JOE. Worst in Mexico.

SLIM. Yeah, the worst, and I wasn't doing anything.

JOE. Horse manure. You'd just pilfered some of the Generalissimo's finest smoking cigars from his humidor.

SLIM. Yeah, I got cracked over the head for *that,* and they never even called me a name when you and I set fire to the Saw Mill in Tacoma.

JOE. Now, I wouldn't say we were there when it happened.

SLIM. We did it.

JOE. We *might* have done it. Or some benevolent friend of the labor movement in this country might have done it.

SLIM. Well, I was there.

JOE. I'm not certain anymore I was.

SLIM. But old—what was his name—he took the rap for us while we were having our good times.

JOE. (*Suddenly angry.*) We had our "good times," Slim, in case your memory has sadly failed, because people were sick and underpaid and out of work and owing money and scared, they were scared all the time, scared you looked in their eyes, sweating at night in bed, sweating in the morning.

SLIM. What was his name?

JOE. He could hardly say. Natase Bomchik. A hunkie.

SLIM. He could never pronounce a word to us and he took the rap.

JOE. I don't remember for what.

SLIM. When you inserted the crow bar in the winches on the San Francisco job and the wheel slipped and crashed through the pier and the dock was shut down for two weeks while every available man got a paying job trying to get the cog out of the mud.

JOE. (*Amazed and happy.*) Wooo, I'd almost forgotten that one.

SLIM. Bomchik took the chains for that one.

JOE. You think I don't remember?

SLIM. It don't pay to forget.

JOE. It's just I don't remember-remember, for all the records.

SLIM. We don't have none, Joe. We're gonna pass without a mark. Except you.

JOE. I'm gonna pass without a mark.

SLIM. That's what I wanted to ask you.

JOE. How could I forget Bomchik there on the siding? We all talked and some bull who didn't like the way Bomchik parted his hair come over and told us all to make ourselves scarce because radicals had destroyed the winch at the pier.

SLIM. I don't know why, he stood up and bowed politely to the cop

JOE. We went away, Bomchik stayed, he didn't take that train. The bull shot at him, with the intention to kill, but being bad at it, just shattered his hand. So he conched Bomchik on the head a couple of times with the sapper—

SLIM. Must've been a dozen, at least.

JOE. And threw him in jail, without medicine, and they had to keep amputating, first the hand, then the arm, then . . . they cut his heart out, I guess.

SLIM. You and I may be the only ones who remember him. He passed without a mark.

JOE. I don't think we killed him. I couldn't live with that.

SLIM. You're right, there, we didn't. So what are you going to do, old friend?

JOE. Well, I wish we could sit around a fire somewheres and have some thin bean soup and pick beasts out of each other's hair.

SLIM. Those weren't good times.

JOE. I didn't say they were, but I'd rather be there than here. (*Slim has ensconced himself at the piano, sings, while playing.*)

SLIM. (*Second verse of "Closer Walk With Thee."*)
I am weak but thou art strong
Jesus keep me from all wrong
I'll be sat-is-fied as long
As I can walk close with thee.
    (*He stops playing.*)
Want to join in on the last verse?

JOE. I should've mistrusted you long ago. Jerusalem Slim, what kind've a handle is that? That's hobo language for Jesus Christ.

SLIM. It was given me. Your pop was a minister, wasn't he, a pastor reverend father god-botherer?

JOE. I don't have family anymore. I didn't come from anywhere but the movement. I was born there, I've lived there, and I believe I'll die there.

SLIM. I was going to ask you . . . (*Plays and sings; Joe joins after the first line: the final verse of "Closer Walk."*)
Now when this fevered life is o'er
Time for me won't be no more
Lead me, lead me gently o'er
To that shore, o, lead me to that shore.

JOE. (*After a brief pause.*) That song is just a comfort, Slim. It just sounds nice. It makes a person shiver with delight. It don't fill his belly.

SLIM. Like some of yours make a good meal? (*Slim pounds out, without singing, a quick, upbeat chorus of "Rebel Girl." Slim, about the song:*) Now what the hell is that all about?

JOE. Just a romantic rebel song, Slim, with no religion in it.

SLIM. For a big, dumb Swede, you twist around a lot. (*He plays "Closer Walk" softly under:*) We were wondering, which is why I got the money and the votes to see you, have you decided to stand and fight, or die day after tomorrow?

JOE. I hadn't concluded yet. I have an ace or two I might play.

SLIM. A lot of *us* have decided, Joe, it would be better all round if you died. It's not personal; it's as you say, you're one of us, we'll all pass without even scraping the face of anything, but you have them on the run, you know. We can read that in the popular papers as well. When they hang you . . .

JOE. I have the choice of being shot, too.

SLIM. Or shoot you, every one of us ten-cent slumgullians is gonna be that much more important and powerful and dangerous, and you'll have a lot more effect as an organizer, Joe, being dead. So we wish you'd get hung or shot as soon as may be, so we don't lose any of the force of it. (*He stops playing, gets up, embraces Joe, during:*) We love you, Joe; I love you. But it's just got to the point where you only fit with things if people feel, maybe have to taste your blood. That's what we all voted. (*Disengages himself.*) Also, it would be sweet, when you're dead, if you could see if you could get cremated. Orsler, our man in the iron mines, thinks if

34

we could get a pinch of your ashes into, say, two hundred en-
velopes and mail them out, then on May of this year, we can have
your remains poured on every mill town, coal and copper and
iron mine, every plant and company store and installation
anywhere.

JOE. (*Angry.*) You stupid son-of-a-bitch, I want to be sprinkled on
hobo camps and little houses and somewhere in the hills a million
miles from here. I don't want to be found dead in Utah.

SLIM. We'll have your earthly remains taken to another state.

JOE. Is that a promise?

SLIM. A promise.

JOE. Where would you be taking me?

SLIM. Chicago. There's a crematorium in the hills out there, it's
where I'd like to be changed.

JOE. You can't be changed.

SLIM. Well, altered into some usable substance.

JOE. That is the stupidest idea.

SLIM. You can say so, but I don't mean anything to most people,
the way you do.

JOE. Okay. I'll take the matter under advisement.

SLIM. What the hell does that mean?

JOE. I'm not sure. I read it in one of these books. I think it means
that I'll go somewhere and think about it and tell you, but you'll
never know what I really thought, especially about an idea as
loonie as yours.

SLIM. I guess that's all I can ask. People, our old friends, and
friends you never met who'd be your friends and who sing your
songs, they are getting ready to grieve for you.

JOE. Well, I wish I could be there, but I haven't decided. If you
find somebody else better to grieve for, let me know, very soon.

SLIM. Yes, well, I have to go with some of the fellows, now, to
parade by the governor's. We're trying to save your life, too. You
made a lot of work for us. (*Pause.*) Did you kill those two, by the
way? I'm just curious.

JOE. I don't remember.

SLIM. That's fine, also. (*John Dawson, with a picnic basket, appears;
the set-up this time is hobo food out of cans and Dago red; he is joining
them.*)

JOE. Don't gawk, John, this is Jerusalem Slim, an old buddy of
mine from the road. He's got to go, but he'll stay for a bit of food.

35

JOHN. (*Contrite.*) Pleased to meet you. I'm sorry, Joe, I was rude before.

JOE. We all get wound up once in a while. (*As they all eat.*) How's your ma?

JOHN. She bought a black dress and a veil.

SLIM. (*Reaching into his pocket.*) I brung a black tie. It's a little wrinkled, but I know a gal in Demarest who'll iron it flat for me.

JOHN. I got a grown up suit, gray, and it scratches like a son-of-a-bitch.

SLIM. What you got, Joe?

JOE. My same black suit and gray shirt. I only ever had one, if the good people of Utah haven't alienated it to the possession of some other felon. Though it's got a bullet hole in it.

SLIM. We'll get it sewed.

JOHN. You take me on the road with you, Mr. Jerusalem?

SLIM. Why? You got a home.

JOHN. They're forcin' me to change there. I didn't mind before. Joe and me been friends, you know, good friends, till this murder came up, and when they hang Joe and all, he won't be here. I don't like my other friends, and they're forcin' me. I'd like to be on the road.

JOE. You think so because it sounds so great, living out of jungles, soaked with the rain, bein' sick and hungry a lot?

JOHN. That's not how you put it.

SLIM. Joe always made it sound good to me, too, and I was there.

JOE. It's good, if you're of the right temperament.

SLIM. Yeah, poor and thin and angrier than anything else you might be.

JOHN. No, you just got to enjoy it.

SLIM. Listen to him talk.

JOE. Kid talk. You got to drop it all soon—is that what they been forcin' you with—and get to be a man.

JOHN. In actual fact, I don't want to be a man. I want to be about like this for another ten or fifteen years and not have two phaetons, five horses, a house with gables to be painted, a bank account, books, Bessie Mallory, the Irish maid, sweethearts, children, friends I meet only in church, nor do I want to owe nobody money or have it owed me or sign contracts or have people sued, arrested and murdered or throw dirt on me when I'm dead.

JOE. That's not right.

SLIM. That's lonely.

JOHN. (*To Joe.*) You're the most lonely one I ever met.

JOE. That's how I am. I have my friends, but I don't feel as easy as they can be with each other. I'd like that house though, but I'd rattle around in it. Those horses would be swell to have, but I'd probably get to feeling so sorry for them, I'd put them out. I would like an aeroplane, though, an aeroplane and fifty dollars and a map. (*Pause.*) You can't look up to me, son, my mind's not right.

JOHN. You can't say that to me.

JOE. (*About the wine that John is drinking.*) Are you having a little too much of the red?

JOHN. Are you?

JOE. I like a drink now and then.

JOHN. I do, too. (*He starts to cry.*) I don't want nothin' to ever change.

JOE. (*Comforting him, tenderly.*) Well, it's gonna.

SLIM. (*Belting wine also.*) Amen, brother. For the better. For the men and women whose work has been stolen from them and sold by the swell guys.

JOE. It's a hope.

SLIM It's more than that. It's a certainty.

JOE. (*To John.*) What's certain is that things will change for you because you'll get larger and tougher and not feel a whole lot in ten years and you'll acquire some vices to make you forget—and it might be tobacco or hard liquor or malt liquor or you'll womanize or, maybe, you'll become a boss. The spunk just seems to run out of men and the hardness runs in after they've lost a couple rounds and buried a friend or two and been cheated or fired at, and then the body starts to hurt, and it's nice to think . . . I don't know.

JOHN. (*Alert.*) That's the dumbest goddamn thing I've ever heard.

JOE. Is it?

JOHN. Oh, yes sir.

JOE. Good. (*Drinking.*) Good, get mad at me. Slim, a cigar?

SLIM. (*Give him a butt from his pocket. Mock polite.*) A light, m'Lord?

JOE. *Sans doubt.* (*Joe smokes in a leisurely fashion, sips his wine.*) Look at me, I'm enjoying myself. I like this. I could get to love it.

JOHN. You're doing' this to get at me.

JOE. (*Angry.*) No, I'm not. I'm a different person than you think I am. I am going to face the firing squad tomorrow.

37

JOHN. No.

JOE. Yes I am. And I'm going to look them square in the puss.

JOHN. (*Louder.*) NO!

JOE. Oh, yes sir—to help you get along a little better, and to help everyone like you get along a little better.

JOHN. (*Still louder.*) NO!!!!!!!

JOE. You dare not admire me.

JOHN. I GOT NO ONE ELSE, YOU STUPID BASTARD!!!!! (*Dawson has appeared.*)

DAWSON. John, I've warned you about salty speech.

JOE. (*Continuing his mood.*) Ah, the Lady Elizabeth, of one of the city's ranking fiefdoms. To whom do I make out the I.O.U. for the pleasure of your company?

DAWSON. Clean up the fixings, John, and go home. You can see Mr. Hill and Mr. . . .

SLIM. Slim. J. Slim.

DAWSON. Later. (*John silently gathers the picnic up.*)

SLIM. (*Intimately, to Joe.*) I believe, Dr. Hillstrom, I shall lamb it, too. Do give reverend regard to the topic we chinned about, concerning the benefits that might derive from the death of the patient, as opposed to keeping the lonely, but with a gift, but slightly crazy son-of-a-bitch alive.

JOHN. (*To Dawson.*) Joe just said he's gonna let them kill him.

DAWSON. (*In a nice way.*) Is that so?

JOHN. Ask him!

DAWSON. (*To John.*) And what do you think, John, is that a good thing?

JOHN. That's a goddamn stupid question!

DAWSON. You're spending too much time at the courthouse. Your manners have gotten atrocious, and you haven't opened even one of the books you were supposed to read this summer.

JOHN. (*Shouts.*) HE SAID ITS FOR MY OWN GOOD!

DAWSON. People like Mr. Hill always say things like that. Go now, John. Read one of the books you're supposed to.

SLIM. You heard your mother. Let's hop it little master. (*John leaves with Jerusalem Slim.*)

DAWSON. You seem quite comfortable.

JOE. I was having a repast, smoking, thinking. I don't think I belong here.

DAWSON. Utah is not friendly.

JOE. Utah is beautiful. I have never seen so much sky. But

Sweden was beautiful, too, and I left, and California, Washington, Nevada, New York, Illinois, they were all beautiful. I was just never at home. (*Pause.*) Do you want to dance? I have some sentimental stuff I wrote for the dancehalls, but the secret is, I like it best. (*He gets up and puts his arms around her and sings while they dance. She will eventually join him and the tempo will grow more and more rapid as they swirl around.*) [*Note: Any waltz melody will serve here.*]
When I hear that melody, with its rhythmic harmony
Then I feel just like I'd be in a dream entrancing
And I'd like to float through space,
    softly glide from place to place
With the fascinating grace of a fairy dancing:
    Oh, please let me dance this waltz with you
    And look in your dreamy eyes of blue
    Sweet imagination, smooth, gliding sensation
    Oh, love I would die just for dancing this waltz with you.
(*They finish in an intimate embrace.*)
You know I wrote another, "Come and Take a Joy-Ride in My Aeroplane?" It never caught on like the basic waltz, the basic hymn, the ballad . . . I wish I knew.
DAWSON. Don't let them do it!
JOE. I'm scared, darling.
DAWSON. Let's clear this up.
JOE. What's in it for you?
DAWSON. I don't know.
JOE. You see?
DAWSON. You shouldn't save yourself for me, anyway. You should get free because you are Joe Hill.
JOE. Ah, but you don't see, there's a moral to being Joe Hill. I have been shot three times in my life, twice by the citizens of Salt Lake City, and every time I could feel the metal tear into me. I was frightened; I could see my blood running out, I could hear the bones crack, especially the time in the hand, I could hear myself breathing, and I yelled in my head, don't shoot me anymore, it hurts, it rips me up. But that was it. When the bullets come into you—you never been shot, I suppose, or cut badly?—(*She nods her head "no."*) Then you know what Joe Hill is: meat, with a small brain and some feelings. So the whole thing don't matter anyway.
DAWSON. I felt my whole body giving birth to John and William, Junior, and Bessie. I liked that. I knew I was alive in there, I could feel myself stirring about.

JOE. You were giving birth, Elizabeth, you were not adding to your collection of bullets. You were experiencing a small rapture. I have not experienced that ever. Now I never will.

DAWSON. So you are going to die?

JOE. (*In a jolly manner.*) Who says?

DAWSON. My son, John.

JOE. (*Sing song.*) One shoe off and one shoe on.

DAWSON. But really die, Mr. Hill?

JOE. I think I have to, don't you? But you tell them, when I'm dead, they can burn me up and sprinkle me around, That'd be my wish.

DAWSON. As you have made all of *this* the case . . .

JOE. What?

DAWSON. Your dying, Mr. Hill, which you will not allow me to save you from . . .

JOE. I can't allow you to. Don't you see?

DAWSON. Yes, I see. Then I must tell you something, what I wanted myself?

JOE. Was it a nice thing?

DAWSON. Yes, Mr. Hill, First of all, it was Geoffrey . . . what a thing, with a behind, if you'll allow me, like two loaves, and Fredrick, the sober Kraut, a horse about his pleasures, and Clarence, who said he was going to show me a thing or two, and the fellow who had no English who used to sweep the stables, and Rufus, who set me afire until I settled.

JOE. I knew you'd had a turn or two.

DAWSON. A turn? A great fire was lit. Pity my diddle-dumpling son John, Mr. Hill, pity the children who have to clean up after the morbid likes of you. We could've been in love a long time, Mr. Hill, and it would've been so sweet. But you hate it.

JOE. I don't hate it. (*Pause.*) I don't hate it!

DAWSON. Oh, but you do. Pity of a lifetime, Mr. Hill.

JOE. (*Sings as she begins to exit, opening her parasol.*)
That's the Rebel Girl. That's the Rebel Girl.
To the working class she's a precious pearl.
　(*Dawson joins him.*)
She brings courage, pride and joy
To the fighting Rebel Boy.
We've had girls before
But we need some more
In the Industrial Workers of the World

40

For its great to fight for freedom
With a Rebel Girl.
DAWSON. I love you.
JOE. I love you, too.
DAWSON. I won't forget you.
JOE. You bet you won't. (*Dawson exits. Joe stands there for a moment. The Judge and attornies return immediately.*)
JUDGE. Don't move, Mr. Hill. (*To everyone.*) I have just been informed by the governor that he will not authorize another stay of execution, despite letters from heads of European states and thirteen thousand communiques of various sorts, including another appeal from President Wilson.
JOE. (*Through his teeth.*) Woodhead.
JUDGE. He has delivered to me the death warrant and I must now thereon affix my signature and . . . which way, Mr. Hill?
JOE. Firing squad.
JUDGE. Very well, We had made plans for either choice. It is customary for some final words by the sentencee on the occasion of his having lost his cause entirely, as you have done. (*Joe gets up and hands the Judge a piece of legal foolscap with scrawls all over it. The Judge peers a moment, then reads in a mocking tone, emphasizing what he takes to be hill billy rhythms; but the mockery is gentle and finally disappears.*)
My will is easy to decide,
For there is nothing to divide.
My kin don't need to fuss and moan—
Moss does not cling to a rolling stone.
    (*During the next two stanzas, Joe is prepared for execution. He is stripped down to a shirt, his hands tied behind his back and he is bound to his chair. A large paper heart is pinned to his chest.*)
My body?—Oh—If I could choose
I would to ashes it reduce
And let the merry breezes blow
My dust to where some flowers grow.
JOE. (*Interposing.*) I'm not perfectly happy with that last line.
JUDGE. (*Continuing reading.*)
Perhaps some fading flower then
Would come to life and bloom again.
This is my last and final will.
Good luck to all of you—Joe Hill.
    (*Speaking for himself now.*)

41

Perhaps we can clear the courtroom, now, ladies and gentlemen. I don't want any but the intended, Mr. Hill, to catch a stray shot. You are free to watch from the gallery, but there seems to be a great rush for seats, so I would get one now, perhaps put a coat or a hat on it, then get a bite to eat. The Salt Lake City house is featuring today— (*Glances in his papers.*) Mutton with capers or beefsteak and the Palace is featuring some fresh salmon, which I've tried, which came in from Seattle just yesterday by rail. The session, otherwise, is adjourned. (*To the attornies.*) Well done, thou good and faithful servants. (*He gavels the court out of session, and the courtroom is clear, except for the Judge, who sits with his head in his hands. Joe, is completely tied-up.*) I would like some of the salmon, but it doesn't agree with me. Nothing agrees with me as this thing I have winds me down, this tedious, inching cancer.

JOE. Try cheeses. Milk.

JUDGE. I'll take the matter under advisement. (*Joe laughs.*) Why didn't you defend yourself? You had every opportunity?

JOE. I thought I did.

JUDGE. That? That was a botch. I have no idea if you are guilty or innocent, I promise you.

JOE. Oh, I'm guilty, in spirit anyway.

JUDGE. You have shown a great deal of manliness.

JOE. No. I'm shy, that's the reason.

JUDGE. You'll be happy to know you have succeeded in disturbing me. Few things do.

JOE. How would that be?

JUDGE. I don't know. I don't believe you. You're too canny to be a radical, you're too smart to louse up a simple robbery.

JOE. And you may be too smart to be a judge.

JUDGE. No, they found the right place for me.

JOE. Maybe I belong in mine.

JUDGE. No, you see, I can't accept that.

JOE. You think the world has always been pretty much like this.

JUDGE. And it's not going to change the way you propose and no reasonable man thinks so and you are a reasonable man and so you have put us all on, and I don't like it.

JOE. None of my blood will be on your hands.

JUDGE. All of it.

JOE. No, sir.

JUDGE. YES! (*The Judge gets up, slips out of his judicial robe. He is wearing a sweat-stained shirt and big galluses. He wanders down to Joe's level.*) The benefit of my training and experience tells me what things are so, and what are not, what can be dealt with, what must be ignored, what must be, so to speak, embraced.

JOE. That makes it easier, I suppose.

JUDGE. There will be a time when things go easier for the workers and when some things will come about I can't even imagine. We once had slaves in this country.

JOE. You still do, sir.

JUDGE. (*Picks up the guitar, tunes.*) Maybe it doesn't amount to a hill of beans, anyway, what you do, what I do. We'll both be dead in a bit, and you'll be remembered and I won't, and someday my house'll be bulldozed down to make way for another. (*Pause.*) I hate to say this to you, but I really wish I could keep the salmon down, with the mustard sauce. It is so good. (*Plays and sings in a mellow way the second verse of "Rebel Girl."**)

"Yes her hands may be harden'd from labor
And her dress may not be very fine;
But a heart in her bosom is beating
That is true to her class and her kind . . ."

JOE. HORSESHIT! That's *my* damn song!

JUDGE. (*Goes on singing.*)

"And the grafters in terror are trembling
When her spite and defiance she'll hurl.
For the only and thoroughbred Lady
Is the Rebel Girl."

JOE. First you're going to kill me dead so I can be sprinkled about, then you'll steal my songs!

JUDGE.

"That's the Rebel Girl! That's the Rebel Girl
To the working class she's a precious pearl
She brings courage, pride and joy
To the Fighting Rebel Boy"

JOE. I DON'T HAVE TO LISTEN TO THIS. SHOOT ME! ANYTHING IS BETTER THAN YOUR SINGIN'.

JUDGE. (*Continues singing; Joe cannot help himself and joins.*)

"We've had girls before
But we'll have some more

---

* Music for this song is included at back of playbook.

In the Industrial Workers of the World
For it's fun to fight for freedom
With a Rebel Girl."
JOE. (*After a pause, crying out.*) I'm scared. Hold me. Tomorrow I won't have a thing.
JUDGE. (*Comforting him.*) I thought you'd cry out. They all do. That's the way it is. I'll probably cry out. Not as loudly, mind. I'll be sensible. (*A blindfold is put on Joe. The Judge walks back to his dias and puts on his robe as the light narrows on Joe, and fades during:*)
JOE. (*To the squad.*) No, now you don't count it. I'll count it.
VOICE. Ready.
JOE. No, when *I* say fire.
VOICE. Set your weapons!
JOE. FIRE!
VOICE. FIRE! (*Blackout on Joe. The Judge puts his head in his hands a minute, then looks up, alert, and takes an evelope from his desk. He opens it and sprinkles the contents, ashes, over the front of the bench. The ashes dance in the light. Suddenly, the judge wipes his fingers, as though they had something foul on them, on his judicial robes and bangs the gavel.*)
JUDGE. Call the next case. (*Stage flooded with light, attorneys, people: Joe is gone.*)
BAILIFF. (*Disappearing in the clamor.*) Call the State of Utah vs. Smith; also call Cunningham vs. Martin, also, call . . . (*As lights fade, a court assistant sweeps the ashes away.*)

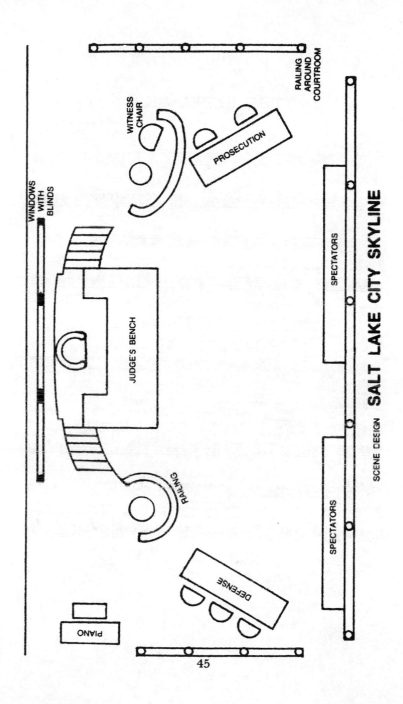

SCENE DESIGN **SALT LAKE CITY SKYLINE**

45

THE REBEL GIRL

Words & Music by
JOE HILL

Copyright, MCMXV, by Wm. D. Haywood

46

The Rebel Girl 1

Music of Joe Hill's "The Rebel Girl."

PROPERTY LIST

ACT ONE

Preset on Defense and Prosecution tables:
legal books
brief-cases
legal pads
pencils
water glasses
carafes of water
Preset on Judge's bench:
a gavel
Bible
personal papers
Personal props:
newspapers (trial spectators)
transcript book (BAILIFF)
parasol and fan (MRS. DAWSON)
smelling salts (MR. JEFFERSON)
guitar, cigarette papers, matches and tobacco (JOE)
notebook (GRUBER)
handcuffs (COURT OFFICER)
Act One Picnic: (JOHN DAWSON)
a basket
checkered tablecloth
linen
napkins
fine china plates
cold chicken
biscuits
fresh fruit
coffee in contemporary-looking vessel

ACT TWO

Preset: same as Act One, but with:
a large number of law books (The Defense Table)
menus and an envelope of ashes (Judge's Bench)
Personal:
brush, shaving, and razor (BAILIFF)

whiskey bottle, black tie, bandana-handkerchief, cigar butt and matches
  (JERUSALEM SLIM)
For the execution:
blindfold
ropes
paper square with a black heart drawn on it
pins
Act Two Picnic: (JOHN DAWSON)
picnic basket
wine in a plain bottle
tin cups
plain bread in a loaf
canned foods without labels
can opener

NEW PLAYS

★ **THE CIDER HOUSE RULES, PARTS 1 & 2 by Peter Parnell, adapted from the novel by John Irving.** Spanning eight decades of American life, this adaptation from the Irving novel tells the story of Dr. Wilbur Larch, founder of the St. Cloud's, Maine orphanage and hospital, and of the complex father-son relationship he develops with the young orphan Homer Wells. "…luxurious digressions, confident pacing…an enterprise of scope and vigor…" –*NY Times*. "…The fact that I can't wait to see Part 2 only begins to suggest just how good it is…" –*NY Daily News*. "…engrossing…an odyssey that has only one major shortcoming: It comes to an end." –*Seattle Times*. "…outstanding…captures the humor, the humility…of Irving's 588-page novel…" –*Seattle Post-Intelligencer*. [9M, 10W, doubling, flexible casting] PART 1 ISBN: 0-8222-1725-2 PART 2 ISBN: 0-8222-1726-0

★ **TEN UNKNOWNS by Jon Robin Baitz.** An iconoclastic American painter in his seventies has his life turned upside down by an art dealer and his ex-boyfriend. "…breadth and complexity…a sweet and delicate harmony rises from the four cast members…Mr. Baitz is without peer among his contemporaries in creating dialogue that spontaneously conveys a character's social context and moral limitations…" –*NY Times*. "…darkly funny, brilliantly desperate comedy…TEN UNKNOWNS vibrates with vital voices." –*NY Post*. [3M, 1W] ISBN: 0-8222-1826-7

★ **BOOK OF DAYS by Lanford Wilson.** A small-town actress playing St. Joan struggles to expose a murder. "…[Wilson's] best work since *Fifth of July*…An intriguing, prismatic and thoroughly engrossing depiction of contemporary small-town life with a murder mystery at its core…a splendid evening of theater…" –*Variety*. "…fascinating…a densely populated, unpredictable little world." –*St. Louis Post-Dispatch*. [6M, 5W] ISBN: 0-8222-1767-8

★ **THE SYRINGA TREE by Pamela Gien.** Winner of the 2001 Obie Award. A breathtakingly beautiful tale of growing up white in apartheid South Africa. "Instantly engaging, exotic, complex, deeply shocking…a thoroughly persuasive transport to a time and a place…stun[s] with the power of a gut punch…" –*NY Times*. "Astonishing…affecting …[with] a dramatic and heartbreaking conclusion…A deceptive sweet simplicity haunts THE SYRINGA TREE…" –*A.P.* [1W (or flexible cast)] ISBN: 0-8222-1792-9

★ **COYOTE ON A FENCE by Bruce Graham.** An emotionally riveting look at capital punishment. "The language is as precise as it is profane, provoking both troubling thought and the occasional cheerful laugh…will change you a little before it lets go of you." –*Cincinnati CityBeat*. "…excellent theater in every way…" –*Philadelphia City Paper*. [3M, 1W] ISBN: 0-8222-1738-4

★ **THE PLAY ABOUT THE BABY by Edward Albee.** Concerns a young couple who have just had a baby and the strange turn of events that transpire when they are visited by an older man and woman. "An invaluable self-portrait of sorts from one of the few genuinely great living American dramatists…rockets into that special corner of theater heaven where words shoot off like fireworks into dazzling patterns and hues." –*NY Times*. "An exhilarating, wicked…emotional terrorism." –*NY Newsday*. [2M, 2W] ISBN: 0-8222-1814-3

★ **FORCE CONTINUUM by Kia Corthron.** Tensions among black and white police officers and the neighborhoods they serve form the backdrop of this discomfiting look at life in the inner city. "The creator of this intense…new play is a singular voice among American playwrights…exceptionally eloquent…" –*NY Times*. "…a rich subject and a wise attitude." –*NY Post*. [6M, 2W, 1 boy] ISBN: 0-8222-1817-8

DRAMATISTS PLAY SERVICE, INC.
440 Park Avenue South, New York, NY 10016 212-683-8960 Fax 212-213-1539
postmaster@dramatists.com www.dramatists.com

NEW PLAYS

★ **A LESSON BEFORE DYING by Romulus Linney, based on the novel by Ernest J. Gaines.** An innocent young man is condemned to death in backwoods Louisiana and must learn to die with dignity. "The story's wrenching power lies not in its outrage but in the almost inexplicable grace the characters must muster as their only resistance to being treated like lesser beings." *–The New Yorker.* "Irresistable momentum and a cathartic explosion...a powerful inevitability." *–NY Times.* [5M, 2W] ISBN: 0-8222-1785-6

★ **BOOM TOWN by Jeff Daniels.** A searing drama mixing small-town love, politics and the consequences of betrayal. "...a brutally honest, contemporary foray into classic themes, exploring what moves people to lie, cheat, love and dream. By BOOM TOWN's climactic end there are no secrets, only bare truth." *–Oakland Press.* "...some of the most electrifying writing Daniels has ever done..." *–Ann Arbor News.* [2M, 1W] ISBN: 0-8222-1760-0

★ **INCORRUPTIBLE by Michael Hollinger.** When a motley order of medieval monks learns their patron saint no longer works miracles, a larcenous, one-eyed minstrel shows them an outrageous new way to pay old debts. "A lightning-fast farce, rich in both verbal and physical humor." *–American Theatre.* "Everything fits snugly in this funny, endearing black comedy...an artful blend of the mock-formal and the anachronistically breezy...A piece of remarkably dexterous craftsmanship." *–Philadelphia Inquirer.* "A farcical romp, scintillating and irreverent." *–Philadelphia Weekly.* [5M, 3W] ISBN: 0-8222-1787-2

★ **CELLINI by John Patrick Shanley.** Chronicles the life of the original "Renaissance Man," Benvenuto Cellini, the sixteenth-century Italian sculptor and man-about-town. Adapted from the autobiography of Benvenuto Cellini, translated by J. Addington Symonds. "[Shanley] has created a convincing Cellini, not neglecting his dark side, and a trim, vigorous, fast-moving show." *–BackStage.* "Very entertaining...With brave purpose, the narrative undermines chronology before untangling it...touching and funny..." *–NY Times.* [7M, 2W (doubling)] ISBN: 0 8222 1808-9

★ **PRAYING FOR RAIN by Robert Vaughan.** Examines a burst of fatal violence and its aftermath in a suburban high school. "Thought provoking and compelling." *–Denver Post.* "Vaughan's powerful drama offers hope and possibilities." *–Theatre.com.* "[The play] doesn't put forth compact, tidy answers to the problem of youth violence. What it does offer is a compelling exploration of the forces that influence an individual's choices, and of the proverbial lifelines—be they familial, communal, religious or political—that tragically slacken when society gives in to apathy, fear and self-doubt..." *–Westword.* "...a symphony of anger..." *–Gazette Telegraph.* [4M, 3W] ISBN: 0-8222-1807-0

★ **GOD'S MAN IN TEXAS by David Rambo.** When a young pastor takes over one of the most prestigious Baptist churches from a rip-roaring old preacher-entrepreneur, all hell breaks loose. "...the pick of the litter of all the works at the Humana Festival..." *–Providence Journal.* "...a wealth of both drama and comedy in the struggle for power..." *–LA Times.* "...the first act is so funny...deepens in the second act into a sobering portrait of fear, hope and self-delusion..." *–Columbus Dispatch.* [3M] ISBN: 0-8222-1801-1

★ **JESUS HOPPED THE 'A' TRAIN by Stephen Adly Guirgis.** A probing, intense portrait of lives behind bars at Rikers Island. "...fire-breathing...whenever it appears that JESUS is settling into familiar territory, it slides right beneath expectations into another, fresher direction. It has the courage of its intellectual restlessness...[JESUS HOPPED THE 'A' TRAIN] has been written in flame." *–NY Times.* [4M, 1W] ISBN: 0-8222-1799-6

DRAMATISTS PLAY SERVICE, INC.
440 Park Avenue South, New York, NY 10016 212-683-8960 Fax 212-213-1539
postmaster@dramatists.com www.dramatists.com

NEW PLAYS

★ **THE CREDEAUX CANVAS by Keith Bunin**. A forged painting leads to tragedy among friends. "There is that moment between adolescence and middle age when being disaffected looks attractive. Witness the enduring appeal of Prince Hamlet, Jake Barnes and James Dean, on the stage, page and screen. Or, more immediately, take a look at the lithe young things in THE CREDEAUX CANVAS..." *–NY Times*. "THE CREDEAUX CANVAS is the third recent play about painters...it turned out to be the best of the lot, better even than most plays about non-painters." *–NY Magazine*. [2M, 2W] ISBN: 0-8222-1838-0

★ **THE DIARY OF ANNE FRANK by Frances Goodrich and Albert Hackett, newly adapted by Wendy Kesselman**. A transcendently powerful new adaptation in which Anne Frank emerges from history a living, lyrical, intensely gifted young girl. "Undeniably moving. It shatters the heart. The evening never lets us forget the inhuman darkness waiting to claim its incandescently human heroine." *–NY Times*. "A sensitive, stirring and thoroughly engaging new adaptation." *–NY Newsday*. "A powerful new version that moves the audience to gasps, then tears." *–A.P.* "One of the year's ten best." *– Time Magazine*. [5M, 5W, 3 extras] ISBN: 0-8222-1718-X

★ **THE BOOK OF LIZ by David Sedaris and Amy Sedaris**. Sister Elizabeth Donderstock makes the cheese balls that support her religious community, but feeling unappreciated among the Squeamish, she decides to try her luck in the outside world. "...[a] delightfully off-key, off-color hymn to clichés we all live by, whether we know it or not." *–NY Times*. "Good-natured, goofy and frequently hilarious..." *–NY Newsday*. "...[THE BOOK OF LIZ] may well be the world's first Amish picaresque...hilarious..." *–Village Voice*. [2M, 2W (doubling, flexible casting to 8M, 7W)] ISBN: 0-8222-1827-5

★ **JAR THE FLOOR by Cheryl L. West**. A quartet of black women spanning four generations makes up this hilarious and heartwarming dramatic comedy. "...a moving and hilarious account of a black family sparring in a Chicago suburb..." *–NY Magazine*. "...heart-to-heart confrontations and surprising revelations...first-rate..." *–NY Daily News*. "...unpretentious good feelings...bubble through West's loving and humorous play..." *–Star-Ledger*. "...one of the wisest plays I've seen in ages...[from] a master playwright." *–USA Today*. [5W] ISBN: 0-8222-1809-7

★ **THIEF RIVER by Lee Blessing**. Love between two men over decades is explored in this incisive portrait of coming to terms with who you are. "Mr. Blessing unspools the plot ingeniously, skipping back and forth in time as the details require...an absorbing evening." *–NY Times*. "...wistful and sweet-spirited..." *–Variety*. [6M] ISBN: 0-8222-1839-9

★ **THE BEGINNING OF AUGUST by Tom Donaghy**. When Jackie's wife abruptly and mysteriously leaves him and their infant daughter, a pungently comic reevaluation of suburban life ensues. "Donaghy holds a cracked mirror up to the contemporary American family, anatomizing its frailties and miscommunications in fractured language that can be both funny and poignant." *–The Philadelphia Inquirer*. "...[A] sharp, eccentric new comedy. Pungently funny...fresh and precise..." *–LA Times*. [3M, 2W] ISBN: 0-8222-1786-4

★ **OUTSTANDING MEN'S MONOLOGUES 2001–2002 and OUTSTANDING WOMEN'S MONOLOGUES 2001–2002 edited by Craig Pospisil**. Drawn exclusively from Dramatists Play Service publications, these collections for actors feature over fifty monologues each and include an enormous range of voices, subject matter and characters. MEN'S ISBN: 0-8222-1821-6 WOMEN'S ISBN: 0-8222-1822-4

DRAMATISTS PLAY SERVICE, INC.
440 Park Avenue South, New York, NY 10016 212-683-8960 Fax 212-213-1539
postmaster@dramatists.com www.dramatists.com